# The GIFTS of CHRISTMAS

*What Will You Give to the Savior?*

*Written by Kathryn Jenkins Gordon*
*Designed by Michelle Fryer*

Cover design copyright © 2016 by Covenant Communications, Inc.
Published by Covenant Communications, Inc.
American Fork, Utah

Printed in China
First Printing: October 2016

22 21 20 19 18 17 16    10 9 8 7 6 5 4 3 2 1

ISBN-13: 978-1-52440-118-4

# The GIFTS of CHRISTMAS

*What Will You Give to the Savior?*

One of the most universal symbols associated with Christmas is gifts—we carefully consider exactly what each should be, wandering through store aisles, wrapping each in brightly colored papers and bows, tucking each beneath the boughs of the evergreen tree in eager anticipation of that breathtaking morning. With each gift, we give a piece of ourselves to a beloved recipient—a piece that speaks volumes of our appreciation and adoration.

Among the gifts you give this year, please consider a gift of yourself to the One who has given you everything. Every day, not just at this Christmas season, you are an innkeeper who decides if there is room for Jesus. And every day, starting with this Christmas season, you can give Him a gift—not one swathed in wrapping and tinsel, but one that lets Him know that in your heart, there will always be room.

Think first of what He has done for you. Elder Jeffrey R. Holland put it beautifully when he said, "The 'good news' was that death and hell could be escaped, that mistakes and sins could be overcome, that there was hope, that there was help, that the insoluble was solved, that the enemy had been conquered. The good news was that everyone's tomb could one day be empty, that everyone's soul could again be pure, that every child of God could again return to the Father who gave them life."

Ours is a debt almost too great to fathom, yet He asks so little of us in return. So this Christmas, start by thinking of something you can do throughout the next year for Him—He who continues to give all to you. This Christmas, set apart a special gift for Him so that *you* can become a special gift for Him.

The pages that follow contain suggestions from which you can choose. There are others that may also occur to you; search your heart until you find exactly what you want to give. Then write your gift on a card and tuck it away. Periodically throughout the year, read what you have written to remind yourself of what you agreed to offer—to make sure that now, and always, there is room for Him in your heart, that your discipleship continues to demonstrate your love for the Savior whose birth we celebrate.

> *"Knowing what we know, how much more do we want to give Him something? But He seems to have everything. Well, not quite. He doesn't have you with Him again forever, not yet. I hope you are touched by the feelings of His heart enough to sense how much He wants to know you are coming home to Him. You can't give that gift to Him in one day, or one Christmas, but you could show Him today that you are on the way."*
>
> —PRESIDENT HENRY B. EYRING

President Ezra Taft Benson once said that when we pass through the veil, nothing will startle us more than how familiar the Father's face is to us. President Henry B. Eyring built on that stunning concept when he explained how we obtain that familiarity: "When you see Him, you will know His voice, because you will have prayed, listened, obeyed, and come to share the thoughts and intents of His heart. You will have drawn nearer to Him." It is through prayer—constant, fervent, diligent prayer—offered through the great Mediator, Jesus Christ, that we come to know that God lives. He is our Father, and He cares for us. And He invites all to come; none is turned away. He is waiting anxiously for the chance to answer your prayers. Approach Him, listen carefully, and He promises, "I will pour out my Spirit upon you, and great shall be your blessing" (D&C 19:38).

> "One can pray and yet not really pray. Prayers can be routinized and become very superficial. When this happens, there is very little communication and very little growth. Yet, given the times in which we live, improving our prayers should be one of our deepest desires if we are genuinely serious about growing spiritually."
>
> —ELDER NEAL A. MAXWELL

# PRAY *with* SINCERITY

# STUDY *the* SCRIPTURES DAILY

Of all the study we can do, of all the things in which we can invest our time, the scriptures are the most profitable. The Lord has assured us that if we ask then seek then knock (see Luke 11:9), we will receive. The asking and seeking take place in the pages of the scriptures; the answers are there, as is the witness that Jesus is the Christ, the Son of the living God. President Howard W. Hunter assured us, "When you have worries and challenges, face them by turning to the scriptures and the prophets." Our daily study yields up a spiritual roadmap that leads us safely and surely through the obstacles of mortality, that sets and keeps us on the path leading to eternal life. As we study diligently, we find ourselves exactly where the Lord wants us to be. His words, scattered across the pages of the standard works, are like letters from home—and in our reading of them, we demonstrate to the

> "Scriptures are like packets of light that illuminate our minds and give place to guidance and inspiration from on high."
>
> —ELDER RICHARD G. SCOTT

Savior that He holds significant real estate in our hearts and that we do, indeed, intend to return home. As Elder D. Todd Christofferson taught, "The scriptures enlarge our memory by helping us always to remember the Lord and our relationship to Him and the Father."

In *Standing for Something*, President Gordon B. Hinckley wrote, "Love is the very essence of life. . . . Love is the security for which children weep, the yearning of youth, the adhesive that binds marriage, and the lubricant that prevents devastating friction in the home. . . . Love, like faith, is a gift of God." In receiving that gift, we receive a force that helps us become more like Christ, who is our perfect example. And in expressing love, in giving that gift back to Him, we erase the differences between all of us who are struggling to work out our salvation. We bridge the chasms of long-ago arguments as well as fresh hurts. We come together as the Savior sees us: none less cherished, none less treasured, none less loved than another. We help all around us to a virtue that is, as President Hinckley said, "like the North Star. In a changing world, it's always constant." And we, in giving that love, offer a constant heart to the Savior.

> "A new commandment I give unto you, That ye love one another; as I have loved you, that ye also love one another."
>
> —JOHN 13:34

# LOVE
*your* NEIGHBOR
*as Yourself*

*Recognize Specific*

# BLESSINGS
# EVERY DAY

Of all people, we are most blessed—but we are not always good at recognizing the blessings with which the Lord demonstrates His love for us. That can be especially true during times when we are struggling or when the winds of adversity howl in their fury. Even then, our blessings outweigh any sorrows. Especially then, our gift of a grateful heart shows our appreciation to a generous Savior. Every day, ask yourself how the Savior blessed you that day. Then, as President Henry B. Eyring said, "If you do that long enough and with faith, you will find yourself remembering blessings. And sometimes you will have gifts brought to your mind which you failed to notice during the day, but which you will then know were a touch of God's hand in your life." In offering that gift to the Savior, we must be sure to show our love by counting our blessings—and then, in His name, by making our blessings count.

> "*When you walk with gratitude, . . . you walk with a spirit of thanksgiving that is becoming to you and will bless your lives. Sincerely giving thanks not only helps us recognize our blessings, it also unlocks the doors of heaven and helps us feel God's love.*"
>
> —PRESIDENT GORDON B. HINCKLEY

The Sabbath day is one of the Lord's most magnificent gifts to us—and only when we honor and appreciate the Savior can we fully honor and appreciate what He has given us. How we treat the Sabbath reveals much about our feelings for Him. The Sabbath is His invitation to each of us: "Come unto me, all ye that labour and are heavy laden, and I will give you rest. . . . For my yoke is easy, and my burden is light" (Matthew 11:28–30). As a gift to the Savior, we might reverence that invitation by determining what we bring to the Lord's table each Sabbath day; even if all we have to offer is a broken heart or a broken life, we express our trust that He can work miracles with broken things. We covenant that we are still with Him. Each Sabbath, we might celebrate that covenant by making the day a measure of our devotion to Him—by appropriately recharging both body and spirit so we might be better, more effective servants. The Lord established the Sabbath as a tangible reminder of His love for us—and in return, we can sanctify that day as a tangible reminder of our love for Him.

> "*Remember the sabbath day, to keep it holy.*"
>
> —EXODUS 20:8

# KEEP *the* SABBATH DAY HOLY

*Have a*
# HUMBLE
# HEART

One of the most meaningful gifts we could give the Savior is that of a humble heart—a heart that is meek, submissive, responsive to the will of God. A humble heart is a heart that cares more about what the Lord thinks than what man thinks. It is a heart that is tuned more to the whisperings of the Holy Spirit than to the shouting and chaos of the world. It is a heart that values the revelations of God over the reasoning of men. It is a heart that conquers pride, that shuns the attitude of those who "seek their own, not the things which are Jesus Christ's" (Philippians 2:21). What a gift it is to humble ourselves by loving the Lord, submitting our will to His, and putting Him first in our lives.

> "*Being humble means recognizing that we are not on earth to see how important we can become, but to see how much difference we can make in the lives of others.*"
>
> —PRESIDENT GORDON B. HINCKLEY

In the relatively short period of time the Savior served His earthly ministry, one of the things He was best known for was His tender, unfailing ability to forgive. In very fact, He took upon Himself all the sins that would ever be committed so that all sinners could receive forgiveness. He has asked the same of us, saying, "I, the Lord, will forgive whom I will forgive, but of you it is required to forgive all men" (D&C 64:10). Yet even in the midst of trying to be as He is, we sometimes struggle to forgive another. Listen to the scriptural injunction, spoken by Him to all of us: if we fail to forgive, "neither will your Father which is in heaven forgive your trespasses" (Mark 11:26). Each of us desperately wants our Father to forgive us, so how wrong it is of us to withhold forgiveness from another! As a gift to He who advocates our cause, perhaps the choice to forgive—not once, not twice, but "seventy times seven," and more—would demonstrate our determination to exercise a largeness of spirit, to believe that all people can change and improve as He desires us to do.

> "*The Savior's Atonement is not just for those who need to repent; it is also for those who need to forgive.*"
>
> —ELDER KEVIN R. DUNCAN

# FORGIVE
*Quickly and Willingly*

Joseph Smith, the Prophet of the Restoration, assured us from the very beginning, "Whatever God requires is right, no matter what it is, although we may not see the reason thereof until all of the events transpire." Knowing that each of God's laws is right, even though we cannot see the end, gives us every motivation to obey—and that obedience can be a tremendous gift to our Savior. For one thing, it assures Him that we intend to return to live with Him,

> "Therefore blessed are ye if ye shall keep my commandments, which the Father hath commanded me that I should give unto you."
>
> —3 NEPHI 18:14

which is one of the fondest desires of His heart. It also demonstrates to Him that we don't shrink away from the difficult things: Elder Stephen L Richards described keeping the commandments as "the most challenging, dramatic, and vital thing in our lives. It tests every fiber of our beings." When we obey God's every command, we set ourselves apart from the world—just as Noah did when he started building an ark before a single drop of rain fell from the skies. But, like Noah and his courageous little band, we will find ourselves in the end saved, rescued. What a gift for both the Savior and for us.

The Savior provided a sobering perspective when He said, "Inasmuch as ye have done it unto one of the least of these my brethren, ye have done it unto me" (Matthew 25:40). As we travel through mortality, we are surrounded by people in various circumstances, some of whom desperately need to be lifted up, ministered to, encouraged, assisted, and cheered out of despair. You can be the Savior's hands in helping these precious, eternal souls—souls He loves with all His heart. Sometimes the need will be temporal or physical, and the abundance you share will come from the purse or the shelf. At other times, you will be invited by Him to share of your moral and spiritual abundance. As part of this gift, care for yourself—make sure you are ready to accept His invitation to help, whenever and wherever it comes. As President Marion G. Romney said, "Food for the hungry cannot come from empty shelves. Money to assist the needy cannot come from an empty purse. Support and understanding cannot come from the emotionally starved. Teaching cannot come from the unlearned. And most important of all, spiritual guidance cannot come from the spiritually weak."

> "I would that ye should impart of your substance to the poor, every man according to that which he hath, such as feeding the hungry, clothing the naked, visiting the sick and administering to their relief, both spiritually and temporally, according to their wants."
>
> —MOSIAH 4:26

# GIVE *of your*
# ABUNDANCE
## *to Those in Need*

Be of
GOOD
CHEER

They were the first words spoken by the Savior as He walked across the water to His disciples, who were cowering in a wind-tossed ship: "Be of good cheer" (Matthew 14:27). Reflecting his own attitude of joy, President Gordon B. Hinckley instructed us, "In all of living, have much fun and laughter. Life is to be enjoyed, not just endured." Do we do more enduring than enjoying? In remembering the Savior's declaration to "be of good cheer," it may be that we tend to break that commandment more than any other. What of a gift to Christ to be of good cheer—to seek out the beauty, the sunlight in our lives with which He blesses us, instead of focusing on the gathering storm clouds or an elusive desire? We decide whether we will merely endure or whether we will enjoy—seeing the light, losing ourselves in the service of others, and giving the Savior even a fractional piece of what He has given us.

> "And ye cannot bear all things now; nevertheless, be of good cheer, for I will lead you along. The kingdom is yours and the blessings thereof are yours, and the riches of eternity are yours."
>
> —D&C 78:18

Throughout all of scripture and all of modern revelation, the Lord tells us that He wants an honest people. In fact, honesty—the quality of being truthful, sincere, and free of deceit—is a requirement for being invited into the Lord's house. There is a sharp difference between those who are honest and those who are dishonest. The dishonest ask, "What will I get?" The honest ask, "Is it right?" One of the real benefits of such a gift to Christ is that it also becomes a gift to others, those who see and hear and watch us. Our transactions are visible not only to those who are close to us, but to those who watch from a distance—and our own honesty, which we give freely to the Lord, becomes a polar star others can follow, leading them to Christ. As with so many other gifts to the Savior, we become the beneficiary of this one as well: we attain happiness only through cleaving to the truth, by living an honest, righteous life filled with good works. We are told that where our treasure is, there is our heart also (see Matthew 6:21); by giving Him the gift of our honesty, we assure the Savior that our heart is with Him now and always.

> "If we are seeking true happiness in the kingdom of God and wish to accumulate the treasures of heaven, our belief requires that we be honest 'to the core' in everything we do."
>
> —JOHN C. BALDWIN

# Be HONEST
## in All Your Dealings

Be
KIND
to Yourself and Others

One of the Savior's most prominent traits was kindness—a loving, gentle nature that sought the good in others and caused Him to treat them accordingly. When you offer this gift to Him, you recognize that each person you encounter—including yourself—is a much-loved son or daughter of our Father in Heaven. You walk in His shoes in treating each—including you!—with kindness, compassion, and forgiveness. Satan would tear us apart; he plants the seeds of discord and conflict in human hearts, hoping to separate and divide us. The Spirit of God never generates contention or a feeling of strife. When you treat others with kindness, you unite with the Savior in helping to unite His children. You can give the gift of reaching out with true friendship as one who bears His name and one who strives to follow the example He gave as He walked the paths of Judaea.

> "*Why* do any of us have to be so mean and unkind to others? Why can't all of us reach out in friendship to everyone about us? Why is there so much bitterness and animosity? It is not a part of the gospel of Jesus Christ."
>
> —PRESIDENT GORDON B. HINCKLEY

Gaining a testimony—becoming converted—to anything rarely happens overnight. It most often requires a foundation of faith: believing that such a thing is possible, followed by desiring to know the truth and investing great effort in study and prayer. Therein lies the value of the gift: it is something that must be consistently worked at, not a trivial matter that can be lightly obtained. Gaining a testimony of a gospel principle requires that we first live the principle with patience and persistence; as Elder David A. Bednar testified, "Consistently being true to the gospel is the essence of conversion." It requires too that we invite the Spirit to testify—which means that we conduct ourselves in every way so that the Spirit can bear witness to us individually—and that we wait on His power. It's a pattern of testimony that calls for righteous living, a broken heart, and a contrite spirit—all of which are the most worthy of gifts.

> "And when ye shall receive these things, I would exhort you that ye would ask God, the Eternal Father, in the name of Christ, if these things are not true; and if ye shall ask with a sincere heart, with real intent, having faith in Christ, he will manifest the truth of it unto you, by the power of the Holy Ghost. And by the power of the Holy Ghost ye may know the truth of all things."
>
> —MORONI 10:4–5

# GAIN *a* TESTIMONY
## *of a Gospel Principle*

# REPENT
## of a Sin or Weakness

More than two millennia ago, the Savior of all mankind bled from every pore in an isolated grove of olive trees. He took His last breath on a cross on Calvary and rose from His tomb after three days—all of it for you, so you would have the opportunity to return and live with Him again. No matter what you have done, no matter how far you have drifted, everything in the gospel of Jesus Christ teaches that you can change—that you can be helped, that you can be made whole. That is His gift to you. Your gift to Him is to thank Him for His infinite Atonement by using it to become clean and pure. This is yet another gift that tremendously blesses the giver, for it lifts from us the heavy burden of sin, the most dire cross we can bear. He already bore that cross for every one of us, making it possible for us to be free of its awful weight, and we show our gratitude through the supernal act of repentance.

> *"However late you think you are, however many chances you think you have missed, however many mistakes you feel you have made or . . . however far from home and family and God you feel you have traveled, I testify that you have not traveled beyond the reach of divine love. It is not possible for you to sink lower than the infinite light of Christ's Atonement shines."*
>
> —ELDER JEFFREY R. HOLLAND

Our Father's great eternal plan of happiness specified that we make our mortal sojourn within a family, one that will continue everlastingly. Even the youngest Primary child sings with vigor, expressing faith that the Lord has shown us how we can be with our families for all eternity (see "Families Can Be Together Forever," *Hymns*, 300). President Gordon B. Hinckley declared definitively that "God is the designer of the family," and it is in the family unit that we recognize the greatest joy, the deepest love, the most cherished associations. As we think of those we cherish most, we realize that it would not be "heaven" without them around us forever. Perhaps your gift to the Savior could be a determined effort to build the kind of relationships with your family members that will endure— creating a place we all want to be with those we love, now and always.

> "Imagine how our own families, let alone the world, would change if we vowed to keep faith with one another, strengthen one another, look for and accentuate the virtues in one another, and speak graciously concerning one another. Imagine the cumulative effect if we treated each other with respect and acceptance, if we willingly provided support. Such interactions practiced on a small scale would surely have a rippling effect throughout our homes and communities and, eventually, society at large."
>
> PRESIDENT GORDON B. HINCKLEY

Build
# ETERNAL
# FAMILY
*Relationships*

*Regularly*
# ATTEND
*the* TEMPLE

The spirit world teems with those who did not hear the gospel message in mortality—and now, having accepted it, prayerfully wait for one of us to enter a temple of the Lord and perform the proxy works for them that they cannot do for themselves. Few things on earth have greater significance and are more important than the work performed in the temple, and the Lord invites us to come to His holy house and participate with Him as saviors of those souls. Our willingness to be worthy of that invitation and to respond by regularly participating in temple work is an outward indication of our love for Him. Through temple worship, we demonstrate to the Lord

> "And inasmuch as my people build a house unto me in the name of the Lord, and do not suffer any unclean thing to come into it, that it be not defiled, my glory shall rest upon it; Yea, and my presence shall be there, for I will come into it, and all the pure in heart that shall come into it shall see God."
>
> —D&C 97:15–16

that we intend to return and live with Him. And as with so many other gifts we give, we too are the recipients of the goodness of this gift. In the temple, we find balm to our souls, an infusion of peace, and help for every problem we could ever imagine. Most of all, we find the holiness that comes with a close communion with our Father and the Savior—something that is ours to enjoy as often as we take the time to attend the temple.

With full-time missionaries flooding the earth in unprecedented numbers, you may feel you have nothing to add—but one of the greatest gifts you can give the Lord is to share His gospel with those around you. He needs you to get up in the morning, to do His work, to open a dialogue, to share His message. It will not always be easy, because salvation never was easy. But in giving this gift, you embrace the Savior's calling when He said, "And if they desire to take upon them my name with full purpose of heart, they are called to go into all the world to preach my gospel unto every creature" (D&C 18:28). Take His name upon you with full purpose of heart, and share the light of His restored gospel with "every creature" in your corner of the world. By doing so, you demonstrate to Him your unfailing faith in Him and in His message.

> *"You have been sent to earth in this dispensation of time because of who you are and what you have been prepared to do!"*
>
> —SISTER LINDA K. BURTON

# TRUST *in* *the* LORD

Sometimes life is hard. Sometimes it's simply hard to keep moving, to keep rejoicing, even to keep living. At times like that, it can be hard—if not impossible—to see the silver lining in the clouds that threaten to overtake us. At such times, never forget: the Lord can see the silver lining, because He is the source of all light. Remember that He loves you. Remember that He is cheering for you. Give Him the gift of your trust. Trust Him enough to keep moving, keep rejoicing, and keep living. Show Him by your faith and your determination that you trust in Him, in all the things He has told you. Pray to Him; pour out your heart. Know that if you are broken, you can be mended. Trust that you are in His loving hands and that you will always be there. Believe, with President Gordon B. Hinckley, "it isn't as bad as you sometimes think it is. It all works out. Don't worry. I say that to myself every morning. It all works out in the end. . . . The Lord will not forsake us." And in giving Him the gift of our trust, we signal that we will never forsake Him.

> "Trust in the Lord with all thine heart; and lean not unto thine own understanding. In all thy ways acknowledge him, and he shall direct thy paths."
>
> —PROVERBS 3:5–6

President Spencer W. Kimball taught, "God does notice us, and he watches over us. But it is usually through another person that he meets our needs. Therefore, it is vital that we serve each other in the kingdom." All around us are people the Lord loves with a love that surpasses comprehension, yet He can help them only through us. Ours are the only hands He has in this mortal sphere; ours are His only feet. In giving a gift of much-needed time, service, temporal support, or spiritual sustenance, we give Him an invaluable gift as well, for "When ye are in the service of your fellow beings ye are only in the service of your God" (Mosiah 2:17). And in the end, there are three who are blessed, for as the poet Ralph Waldo Emerson wrote, "It is one of the most beautiful compensations of life that no man can sincerely try to help another without helping himself." We realize the sacred promise that by losing ourselves, we miraculously find ourselves—and engrave more deeply than ever the name written always in our hearts.

> *"In the Lord's service the path is not always easy. It often requires sacrifices, and we will likely experience adversity. But in serving Him, we discover that His hand is truly over us."*
>
> —ELDER ROBERT D. HALES

# *Be* HIS HANDS

# MAKE
*a* GOAL
*and Reach It*

When you have a goal—whether spiritual or temporal—and you are working toward reaching it, you will find that exhilarating things start happening in your life. You become absorbed in doing things that make a difference. You invest your energy in a worthwhile purpose. Your life moves forward in a positive direction. You become what you think about and what you strive to achieve. If you already have a goal, make this the year to reach it. If you still need to set a goal, pray and ponder about what the Savior would like you to accomplish, then design a plan and start working. As you work on that gift, remember the sage advice of President Gordon B. Hinckley: "You have not failed until you quit trying." Even if your end result is not perfect, you will grow from the effort and be a little better than you are now—a step closer to returning to your heavenly home with honor.

> "*We* can become the masters of our own destinies by practicing self-discipline, by setting worthy goals that will lead to higher ground so that we can become what our Heavenly Father wants us to become."
>
> —ELDER M. RUSSELL BALLARD

The Savior has been called the Prince of Peace, and He has repeatedly promised peace to those who follow Him. To His disciples, He vowed, "Peace I leave with you, my peace I give unto you: not as the world giveth, give I unto you. Let not your heart be troubled, neither let it be afraid" (John 14:27). You can give Him the gift of promoting peace by doing what He wants; we pave the way for peace when we love the things of God more than the things of the world. You can give the gift of peace by forgiving what needs to be forgiven, by forgetting what needs to be forgotten, by choosing the way of serenity and goodwill. Both inner and outer peace will come as we covenant to follow the Lord, to accept His values in every thought and act, in every way of life. Your gift to Him whose name is written on your heart is to promote the peace for which He gave His life. Through your gift of becoming a peacemaker, you will, as promised, be called a child of God (see Matthew 5:9).

> *"I hope you will go out today looking for opportunities to do as He did and to love as He loves you. I can promise you the peace that you felt as a child will come to you often and it will linger with you."*
>
> —PRESIDENT HENRY B. EYRING

PROMOTE
PEACE

*Walk the Savior's*
# PATH *of*
# CHARITY

In listing the virtues He most wants us to have, the Savior identified one—charity—as "the greatest of these" (1 Corinthians 13:13). How He would rejoice in the gift of charity, a gift that makes us not just one who arrives with a casserole but one who supports, teaches, and believes in another. Elder Marvin J. Ashton gave a masterful definition of charity, in which he included being kind; refusing to judge or categorize another; giving the benefit of the doubt; accepting another's differences, weaknesses, and shortcomings; being willing to forgive one who has hurt us; resisting the impulse to become offended; and having patience with one who lets us down. "None of us need one more person bashing or pointing out where we have failed or fallen short," he taught. "Most of us are already well aware of the areas in which we are weak. What each of us does need is . . . [people] who support us, . . . who believe we're trying the

> "Charity suffereth long, and is kind; charity envieth not; charity vaunteth not itself, is not puffed up, Doth not behave itself unseemly, seeketh not her own, is not easily provoked, thinketh no evil."
>
> —1 CORINTHIANS 13:4–5

best we can." We can be those people, rooting for and cheering on those who might otherwise feel battered and broken. We can be, as our Savior would want, healers and helpers and cheerleaders along their journey back to Him.

> *"Whatever principle of intelligence we attain unto in this life, it will rise with us in the resurrection. And if a person gains more knowledge and intelligence in this life through his diligence and obedience than another, he will have so much the advantage in the world to come."*
>
> —D&C 130:18–19

When the last textbook is slammed shut and we dance across the graduation stage, our learning is not finished—in fact, it has just begun. The Prophet Joseph Smith cautioned, "A man is saved no faster than he gains knowledge." A meaningful gift to the Savior could be a lifetime pursuit of learning. In His glorious role as Creator, the Savior provided for us an endless array of plants, animals, rocks, minerals, chemicals, fish, and birds, among other things; we ourselves have developed an almost endless array of peoples, languages, and customs. The list of things for us to learn may be exhaustive, but as Leonardo da Vinci said, "Learning never exhausts the mind." What a compliment to, and gift for, the Savior—to demonstrate interest in what He has given us. Such learning will also bring us to Him, for in addition to books and all the other tools at our disposal, the best way to learn is, as Joseph Smith told us, "to go to God in prayer, and obtain divine teaching."

Become a
# LIFETIME
# LEARNER

# HAVE FAITH
*through Adversity*

Every person who lives on this earth has one thing in common: all of us experience adversity—those storms that howl around us, sometimes with such fury that we fear for our survival. In very fact, such adversity is a gift from our Father and His Son, a divine tutorial that helps us develop the skills we need to receive the greatest gift of all, eternal life. It is evidence of Their infinite love for us. Our gift to Them and the evidence of our love is to demonstrate unremitting faith through adversity, a faith that will banish fear and discouragement and even anger. Our gift is to obey the commandments, to choose the right thing even while the storms rage around us. It is to exercise trust—the trust that the Lord will deliver

> "*My son, peace be unto thy soul; thine adversity and thine afflictions shall be but a small moment; And then, if thou endure it well, God shall exalt thee on high; thou shalt triumph over all thy foes.*"
>
> —D&C 121:7–8

us in His due time, that He truly is the "high priest of good things to come" (Hebrews 9:11).

Who is this Christ, this one to whom we hope to give our finest gift? We promise to remember Him—but even if we forget Him, He always remembers us. Consider what He did for us on Golgotha's hill and what He continues to do for us now. He came to earth and walked the path each of us is called on to walk as part of our mortal sojourn; by doing so, He is uniquely qualified to strengthen us and succor us through even our most grueling circumstances. There is no grief or sorrow or agony we can suffer that He did not suffer first—and none that He cannot take from us, lifting us and healing us in a kind of divine arithmetic that we, with our mortal minds, cannot comprehend. We will never suffer what He did, but we can and must respond to His call to become His disciples. We must never let that call fall on ears deafened by the lure of the world. "There will be days," said President Dieter F. Uchtdorf, "when your hearts are heavy and your heads hang down. Then, please remember, Jesus Christ, the Redeemer, is the Head of this Church. It is His gospel. He wants you to succeed. He gave His life for just this purpose." He offers "the way, the truth, and the life" (John 14:6), and we can offer our full discipleship by making Him our first priority, even when doing so seems impossibly hard. For in the end, if we have not chosen Him, it will not matter what we have chosen.

# *Make* CHRIST
## Your First Priority

"There is not a single loophole or curveball or open trench to fall into for the man or woman who walks the path that Christ walks. When He says, 'Come, Follow Me' (Luke 18:22), He means that He knows where the quicksand is and where the thorns are and the best way to handle the slippery slope near the summit of our personal mountains. He knows it all, and He knows the way. He is the way."

—ELDER JEFFREY R. HOLLAND

*Of all the names on my Christmas list, His should be first—He who gave all to me,*
*He whose life ensures that mine will be everlasting.*
*He asks only that I love as He loved—so my gift of love to Him,*
*represented by a chosen act,*
*engraves His name on my heart this season and always.*